Finding Out About
LIFE IN BRITAIN
IN THE 1950s

Sarah Harris

Batsford Academic and Educational *London*

Contents

© Sarah Harris 1985
First published 1985
Reprinted 1988

Typeset by Tek-Art Ltd, Kent
and printed and bound in Great Britain
by Richard Clay Ltd,
Chichester, Sussex
for the publishers
B.T. Batsford Ltd,
4 Fitzhardinge Street
London W1H 0AH

ISBN 0 7134 4424 X

ACKNOWLEDGMENTS

The Author would like to thank the following for their help in preparing this book: Cora Buckley, Sue and Paul Bush, Graham Davies, Shirley Dewsnap, Nick Harris, Barry Helliwell, Jennie Lee, Dorothy Marsh, Michael Rawcliffe, Sue Taylor and Amy Wood.

The Author and Publishers thank the following for their kind permission to reproduce the illlustrations: BBC Hulton Picture Library, pages 5, 20; Derbyshire County Council, pages 15, 28-29; Gordon Fraser, page 7 (photograph by Charles Walls); Nick Harris, page 10; Godfrey Thomson Unit, University of Edinburgh, page 14. The illustrations on pages 8, 16, 17, 19, 27, 32, 33, 34, 35 are from personal collections. The drawings on pages 6, 39 and 47 are by R.F. Brien.

Cover photos
The colour photograph on the front cover shows the Jodrell Bank Radio Telescope, built for Manchester University in 1957 (J. Arthur Dixon). Jiving photograph: BBC Hulton Picture Library.

Introduction

If you were to ask anyone who remembers the 1950s to sum up, in a single word or phrase, what that decade meant to them, you would probably get a bewildering number of different answers. Many would probably say "The Coronation", but others would reply: "Teddy Boys" or "The Four-Minute Mile" or "Suez" or "Super-Mac and You've Never Had It So Good"; "The Conquest of Everest" or "Rock 'n' Roll".

There is always a difficulty looking at a period of history which isn't packaged neatly into a manageable theme. For the 1950s there is no neat beginning and end, no clear idea of what should be emphasized and what left out. But it means that we can gain a clear sense that people's everyday experiences were as varied, as interesting, as mundane, as sad or as happy as our own, and that should help us view the tidy packages of more distant history with a questioning eye.

Although the rationing imposed during the Second World War was not finally lifted until May 1954, by 1950 the tone of life in Post-War Britain had been set. The Labour Government (1945-51) had extended the Welfare State, most significantly creating the National Health Service. They had firmly established the idea that it was the government's responsibility to manage the economy in order to maintain full employment and had followed a policy in relation to other countries designed to prove that Britain was still a world power, bloodied perhaps by the war, but definitely unbowed.

The Conservative Party, which won the election of 1951 and was to continue in power throughout the decade, followed the same policies. There was a difference of emphasis but not of principle between the parties' programmes during these years – a consensus view that the years before the war, marked by poverty and unemployment, could not be returned to.

In some ways, these policies were successfully implemented. The young people of Britain were better fed, better educated and their health was better cared for than ever before. Unemployment was kept below 500,000 throughout the decade. Consumer goods, such as televisions, washing machines, vacuum cleaners and cars, became much more commonplace. Britain developed her own Hydrogen Bomb, maintained her army and navy all over the world and participated in Summit Meetings with the leaders of the Soviet Union and the United States.

But a lot of this success was superficial. Although many new houses were built, homelessness remained a huge problem; though health care was improved, no new hospitals were built. People were in work, but industrial production failed to improve significantly and investment remained low.

The root of many of these failures lay in the huge amounts Britain spent on defence. Not only did she finance the development of the Hydrogen Bomb and missiles to deliver it to targets, but she also maintained her conventional forces – to share in defending Europe; to fight the Korean War; and, in one embarrassing incident, to invade Egypt – the Suez Crisis of 1956. The struggle for independence in colonies such as Malaya, Kenya and Cyprus placed a further strain on Britain's "defence" budget.

But it really wasn't until the 1960s that people generally began to suspect that things weren't as good as they seemed. During the '50s life was a great deal better than before or even during the war. Just being in work meant affording previously unthought-of luxuries like a summer holiday. The revolution in man-made fibres meant clothes became cheaper and easier to care for and nylon stockings commonplace. It was the decade in which the human race conquered Everest, space and the four-minute mile; in which people felt optimistic as a young queen reigned over a young people (the birth rate remained quite high throughout the 1950s); in which you could jive in the aisles of your local cinema to "Rock Around the Clock"; laugh at the novel humour of the "Goons" on the radio and watch live television coverage of election nights, complete with swing-ometers and computer – all in your own home.

This book looks at these memories of the 1950s as well as some of the conventionally more important events. Whether any or all of these topics prove to be central to our history only time will tell, but I hope they convey a clear sense of what some people found it was like to be living in Britain in the 1950s.

1. PEOPLE
Try to talk to as many people as you can who remember life in the 1950s. It is important to get as wide an age range as you can. People who grew up in the '50s will have different recollections from those who had the responsibility of homes and families, and for people who grew old in the '50s life was very different again.

2. WRITTEN SOURCES
(a) _Documents and Diaries_ Ask the people to whom you talk if they have any mementoes of the 1950s. Press cuttings of Pop Stars, National Service records and school reports are just a few of the items you may be able to obtain. Some people may have kept diaries or letters from that time.
(b) _Newspapers_ Local and National newspapers may be on micro-film in your local library. Don't just read them for the stories. Look at the advertisement pages as well. They can tell you about jobs, houses and goods on sale.
(c) _Autobiographies_ Many politicians and some less prominent people have written about life in the 1950s. These autobiographies can be quite good sources of information.

3. VISUAL MATERIAL
(a) _Buildings_ Wander around your town and try to find the old cinemas and dance halls. Many of them have now been converted to other uses. Perhaps you can find houses, factories or schools built in the 1950s. Look out for dates and try to decide how you recognize a 1950s' building from the design or materials used.
(b) _Maps_ Try to get hold of maps of your area surveyed before 1950 and compare them with more modern ones. It is often possible to identify new building (especially council

The living room of a new house in Northampton, 1951.

building) that took place at that time.

(c) *Objects* Museums sometimes have sections devoted to the 1950s (such as the Castle Museum in York), but a good way to discover what sort of design was fashionable then is to ask someone who was married in the 1950s to show you their wedding presents.

The Festival of Britain

It was not an auspicious moment. There was war in Korea. Rationing was stricter than in wartime. Everybody was in a tired and scratchy mood. To many people the Festival, conceived . . . as a tonic to the nation, seemed more like a lollipop stuck into our mouths to keep us quiet. The press was universally hostile. Conservatives suspected it as a smokescreen for advancing Socialism. Labour dismissed it as . . . middle-class. Luckily we were too busy to listen for the catcalls and in the end, despite strikes, shortages and appalling weather, the South Bank exhibition . . . opened on time within reach of its budget and proved a huge success. (*Hugh Casson, Director of Architecture for the Festival of London,* Hugh Casson, Dent, 1983)

On 3 May 1951 King George VI attended a service of dedication at St Paul's Cathedral which officially opened the Festival of Britain. The decision to hold the Festival had been announced in the House of Commons in December 1947, its purpose to encourage creative effort, to stimulate trade and to mark the centenary of the Great Exhibition of 1851. The centre of the Festival was the South Bank of the Thames in London, where Exhibition Halls were built illustrating the Life of the British People, Industry and Agriculture. A Fun Fair was opened in Battersea Park and special events and celebrations were organized throughout the United Kingdom. By the end of September almost 9 million people had visited the exhibition centre and millions more had been involved in one way or another in what was described as "an act of national autobiography".

The official symbol of the Festival. It shows Britannia upon a rising star. What do you think it was meant to symbolize?

This song was sung by an evangelist preaching on the beach at St Mary's Bay in Kent in the summer of 1951:

O Festival of Britain, what made your
    country great?
Not folks who drink and gamble and
    God's day desecrate.
It was the Christian Gospel
    transformed both men and state.
O Festival of Britain!
Extol the things that made you great.
(Recalled in 1983)

A UNITED COUNTRY

The Festival Hall on the South Bank of the Thames. This is one of the few permanent memorials to the Festival.

One of the projects undertaken by the Festival of Britain Office was to publish new Guide Books to all the areas of Britain. This extract from the introduction to the books gives a good idea of the romantic notion of the unity of Britain, past, present and future, that underlay the Festival.

These guides have been prompted by the Festival of Britain. The Festival shows how the British people, with their energy and natural resources, contribute to civilisation. So the guide-books as well celebrate a European country alert, ready for the future, and strengthened by a tradition which you can see in its remarkable monuments and products of history. . . . It is this living country of today which the guide books emphasise, the place and the people. . . . The aim is to show what Britain is now, in the North, the Midlands and the South, in East Anglia and the West, in Wales, Scotland, Northern Ireland, and to explain something of the why and the wherefore. (*About Britain No.3. Home Counties*)

Imagine you have been asked to provide an exhibit, large or small, to illustrate "The Life of the British People" today. What object would you choose that you feel would help other people understand our lives?

The Coronation

On 2 June 1953 Queen Elizabeth II was crowned in Westminster Abbey. Parts of the ceremony used dated back to the coronation of King Edgar at Bath in 973 and, for the first time, the complex, symbolic rituals of the service could be shared by the people, as the service was televised live and filmed in colour for showing later in the cinemas. The occasion was the excuse for celebration throughout the country and the Commonwealth.

Students in the Domestic Science class at a Derby Secondary Modern School made and decorated their own cakes. One of the designs was of the golden coach used in the coronation, another of the crown. Schools had a holiday for the Coronation, and parties were also held in the streets and old people's homes.

TO REMEMBER IT BY

Schools throughout Britain organized parties and every schoolchild received an official souvenir of the occasion.

> The County Council have now decided on the form of provision to be made for school children in connection with the Coronation.
>
> They will be prepared to bear the cost of one of the following types of souvenirs, if approved by the Council of Industrial Design, for presentation to each child attending a maintained school within the county viz: Mugs and beakers, pencils, badges and brooches, spoons, pottery dishes, or books. If an approved souvenir costs more than 2/– (the maximum approved by the Ministry of Education) the excess cost will have to be met from local sources.... No part of the County Council grant may be spent on the provision of foodstuffs. (*Glossop Chronicle*, 16 January 1953)

Which souvenir would you have chosen for your school?

SENTIMENT

A Popular Song for the Coronation:

> In a golden coach there's a heart of gold
> Riding through Old London Town
> With the sweetest Queen the World's
> ever seen
> Wearing a golden crown.
> As she rides in state through the palace
> gate
> The whole world her beauty can see.
> In a golden coach there's a heart of gold
> That belongs to you and me.

BOROUGH OF GLOSSOP
CORONATION ENTERTAINMENTS
COMMITTEE
Programme of Events
May 30th to June 6th

Saturday May 30th
   2.30pm Official Opening of Coronation Week by the Worshipful the Mayor of Glossop, Alderman R.A. Beckmann, at the Manor Park, Gala Afternoon and Evening, Pet Shows, Punch and Judy, Coconut Shy etc.
   7.30pm Coronation Dance, Victoria Hall, Melochords Band, Licensed Bar, Refreshments, Tickets 3/–

Sunday May 31st
   10.20am Civic Procession to leave the Market Ground for service at the Parish Church at 11am
   3pm and 7pm Concerts by the Besses o' the Barn Band in Manor Park.

Monday June 1st
   2.30pm Novelty Cricket Knockout Competition (three-a-side) at North Road Cricket Ground. Admission 6d.

Tuesday June 2nd
   8pm to 3am The Mayor's Coronation Ball at the Victoria Hall.
   10pm Beacon Fire on Whiteley Nab prepared by local scouts.

Wednesday June 3rd
   3pm Judging of Decorated Streets and Houses.
   7pm Finals of the Borough Coronation Knock-out Competition at Manor Park.
   Tennis Exhibition Matches in Manor Park by J.R. Statham, Derbyshire County Captain and County Champion 1951, W.T. Hough, Derbyshire County Champion 1950, and prominent local players.

Thursday June 4th
   7.30pm Swimming Gala and Polo Match at Woods Baths, Admission 2/– and 1/–.

Friday June 5th
   7.30pm Elizabethan Evening at the Victoria Hall presented by the Townswomen's Guild. Excerpts from "Merrie England" by Edward German; ONE-ACT-PLAY, "The Queen's Ring" by L. du Garde Peach. Seats bookable 3/– and 2/– at Pell's High Street.

Saturday June 6th
   2pm TOWN PROCESSION consisting of Tableaux and Decorated Vehicles entered by local firms, schools etc.
   7pm Chamber of Trade Shopping Week – Winning Tickets to be drawn in Manor Park.
   7.30pm Coronation Dance at the Victoria Hall, Regent Dance Band, Licensed Bar, Refreshments, Tickets 3/– each.
   (from *The Glossop Chronicle*, 22 May 1953)

Try to find the programme of events your town or area organized for the Silver Jubilee in 1977. Did people still enjoy doing the same sort of things?

Housing

THE EXTENT OF THE PROBLEM

When the Second World War began there were 140,000 houses scheduled for demolition. All or nearly all of these were still inhabited. By now the slum houses were probably two or even three times that number. Some experts estimated the total at half a million. It was a terrifying picture. I now proposed with the help of Government grants to induce the local authorities to set about this task at full speed. Materials were coming along, and I felt sure that . . . slum clearance would begin again. But with the best will in the world, in some cities it would take ten, perhaps twenty years to clear the whole mass away. (Harold Macmillan, Minister of Housing 1951-54, in *Tides of Fortune 1945-1955,* Macmillan, 1969)

During the depression of the 1930s and the war very few houses had been built and many had been destroyed in the great "blitzes" on British towns such as London, Coventry and Plymouth. The 1950s opened with a serious housing shortage and efforts were made by governments to build as many houses as fast as possible – both council and private – in an attempt to fill the gap. Though house building did reach new records, the problem had by no means been overcome by the end of the decade.

BEING REHOUSED

We lived in this house in Old Glossop. It had been condemned years before but nothing had ever been done about it. We shared an outside toilet with thirteen other people (it was a big family next door) and paid 8/6d a week rent. Then, about 1952 we got an offer of one of the new flats the council had put up in Queens Drive. 22/6d a week that was. But it was very nice. Had its own bathroom and everything. (Amy Wood, b. 1913)

BUYING A HOUSE

In 1957 we bought a new semi in Sheffield. It was about £2,000. My husband was earning £1,000 a year and we had to pay £15 a month on the mortgage. It was a really big decision. I can remember having heart attacks at the thought of it. (Cora Buckley, b. 1935)

In 1958 I took home £7 a week and my husband £11 so even beginning to think of paying a mortgage out of that was very difficult. (Shirley Dewsnap, b. 1933)

◁ *The flats to which Amy Wood moved, built by Glossop Town Council in the early 1950s.*

HOUSE HUNTING

When you were first married you lived with your in-laws until you could find somewhere to rent. As soon as you heard someone had died you rushed round to the landlord to see if you could have it. (Jenny Lee, b. 1934)

HOUSES FOR SALE

The Hyde Reporter, 27 June 1958:

£75 dep. STALYBRIDGE Compact TERR. lounge, living room, kitchen. 2 beds. modern grate. £230

DENTON, Small TERR. 2 beds., living-room, kitchen price £325

HR. OPENSHAW. Well-built modernised HOUSE, 2 beds., (one with bath installed), hall, lounge dining-room, built-on kitchenette £575

MARPLE BRIDGE: Attractive Mod. SEMI DET. HOUSE, containing hall, sitting-room, kit., pantry, 2 beds., bathroom and w.c.; £1,200

MARPLE, Modern detached, good-size gardens. Built-on garage. Hall, lounge, dining room (each with bay), kitchen, 3/4 good bedrooms, bathroom, sep. w.c. Part centrally heated. £2,750

What can you notice about the advertisements for the cheaper houses?

During the 1950s automatic aids to housework, which had been rare luxuries before the war, became increasingly commonplace. Cleaning the house, feeding and clothing the family became less arduous tasks; the quality of life for many women working in the home improved, and neatly coincided with a change in attitudes to child care. It was becoming fashionable for mothers to spend a great deal of time playing with their children. This was supposed to ensure that children grew up "well-balanced" and more intelligent, with a greater chance of doing well in the new society of post-war Britain.

From The Radio Times, *June 1959. Why should owning a refrigerator have reduced the burden of work for women at home?*

HEAVY, TIRING WASHING DAYS A THING OF THE PAST

NEW Hoover Electric Washing Machine
does the full weekly wash for a large family

The new Hoover Electric Washing Machine saves hours of hard drudgery every week. It washes everything astonishingly quickly and *spotlessly clean*. Works on an entirely new " gentle-with-the-clothes " principle, and is such a handy size it will stand under the average draining board. You will be delighted, too, with the wringer — cleverly sprung to take even large, bulky articles.

So don't wear yourself out any longer. See your Hoover Dealer and order a Hoover Electric Washing Machine *now*. Hire Purchase available.

Remember, it does the full weekly wash for a large family

£25 (plus £6.5.0. tax) Hire Purchase available

And it's made by **HOOVER** TRADE MARK

MAKERS OF THE WORLD'S BEST CLEANER

From The Radio Times, *July 1950.*

DOING THE WASHING

I got a spin dryer for a wedding present [1958]. That was a great innovation. We had a hoover too but the washing machine and the fridge had to wait a few years. . . . They were extras and luxuries – not standard fittings. (Shirley Dewsnap, b. 1933)

Washing machines were a revolution. I got one for my 21st birthday. My Mum and Dad gave me £60 and I got a washing machine. I'd just had Stephen [her son]. They weren't automatic. You still had to stand there. They had hand wringers, though my English Electric had a power wringer – that was wonderful. (Cora Buckley, b. 1934)

A MAN'S VIEW

Don't let anyone kid you Brothers, that we don't welcome automation – we do, but the workers must be in a position to have a say in how automation should be used and to have a fair share of the profits. I don't grumble when I get home from work because my wife has been able to sit down in the afternoons because I have bought her a washing machine, a vacuum cleaner and an electric sewing machine. That is the beginning of automation – making the worker's life easier. Has it made your life easier? I doubt it. (Secretary to the National Motor Joint Shop Stewards Committee, June 1956, in a speech to his fellow trade unionists arguing against increased automation in the motor industry.)

Which household appliance do you think would have made the biggest difference to housework? Explain your choice.

13

The 1944 Education Act reorganized all the schools in England and Wales. Children now attended a primary school from the ages of 5 to 11; then they transferred to a secondary school having taken (in the vast majority of cases) a selection examination, called the 11+, which determined which sort of secondary school they would go to – usually either a grammar school (if they "passed") or a secondary modern (if they didn't), although the Act also allowed for a third sector in secondary education – the technical school.

Here are some questions about secret writings or codes. You have to find out how the code is made up – it is different in each question – and then underline the correct answer in the brackets.

Here is an example :–

If NPRS means "team," SPN means (men | mat | set | <u>met</u> | man)

Since NPRS means "team," N must stand for t, P for e, R for a and S for m. In the same code, therefore, SPN must mean "met," and so we have underlined "met" in the brackets. Now do these. Remember there is a different code for each question.

59. If NDGLQ means "strap," then DLG means (rat | pat | tar | rap | tag | sat)

60. If OLNZRXS means "picture," then XLOS means
(rice | pure | rips | curt | ripe | cure)

61. If CVMSHDI means "strange," then VISM means
(team | gate | star | tear | sane | rang)

62. If FNCQDX means "hostel," then FNXD means
(lost | hose | hole | hold | lose | lots)

63. If RGEYSDK means "inspect," then YRGK means
(sect | snip | tins | pink | spit | pint)

64. If NRMZE means "beard," then EMZR means
(bare | darn | dare | dear | bear | read)

65. If YSLOMV means "depart," then MOVS means
(rats | rate | mate | rots | rave | tape)

66. If OKHVCL means "repast," then CHVOK means
(spark | share | shark | spare | chase | shake)

SCHOOL LOG BOOKS

Every Head Teacher has to keep a school log book and these can prove fascinating sources of information, not only about the school but also about the community it serves. This is an extract from the School Log Book for 1957 for Boughton Monchelsea in Kent:

Mar 19
Some 50 parents attended Parents Meeting. The Hall was decorated with vases of daffodils and there was a display of children's miniature gardens. The Headmaster gave a brief survey of the work of the school and then Mr. Chevenix Trench, A.C.E.O. spoke on the 1944 Education Act and Kent. He stressed why it was better to be in a Modern School rather than at the bottom of a grammar school . . .

Jul 5
Class 1 outing to Greenwich. By river to Westminster, went round the Abbey and saw the changing of the Guard at Buckingham Palace. Trevor Fridd led the singing on the bus and climbed the wall of the old Observatory, pea-nuts shells on the floor of Greenwich Museum, and David Edwards trapped his fingers in the coach door, but these were minor incidents.

Jul 16
School beat Loose by 29 runs, David Piper 46 not out and Trevor Fridd 7 for 11.
Thus ended a great cricket season with eight matches played of which we won 3. David Piper had a batting average of 53.5 in 8 innings and Trevor Fridd took 34 wickets for 104 runs. Average 3.0

Nov 29
As the headmaster was leaving for the Boys Grammar School Speech Day came the terrible news of the Oakwood Hospital fire. Mr. J. Hawkes and Mr. A. Farrow both parents and both part-time firemen lost their lives when a tower collapsed. Mr. Latham also on injured list.

Hague Bar Primary School, near New Mills, Derbyshire, about 1953. What strikes you most about the children and the classroom?

RECOLLECTIONS

I went to two completely different primary schools. One was in Worcester Park, in Surrey. It was a new school and in my memory has lots of light and space. We did dance and music and every morning wrote our diaries in which we could draw pictures. My other primary school, in South Wales, was much more crowded, dark and formal. I don't remember ever being allowed to leave our desks, which were in rows. In one class we were seated in order of achievement – boys first (top boy next to the open fire, bottom girl in the coldest corner of the room). We even did our once-a-week painting lesson sitting in our desks. The slipper was used regularly too – even for minor misdemeanours. I quite enjoyed it though. We were always very busy and since I was reasonably good at my work I kept getting gold stars. It can't have been much fun if you weren't good at reading and arithmetic though. (Sarah Harris, b. 1948)

THE ELEVEN PLUS

I shall never forget The Day. It was raining for the first paper. When we arrived at school pens, rulers, pencil cases were taken away and we were issued with a number (I think mine was 49). Then we were given two pencils – I hadn't written with a pencil for years and it seemed very degrading. No-one smiled. The headmaster came in with a large brown envelope. He told everyone that this was the most important day of our lives and that we were to DO OUR BEST. I thought I should die – my hands were so sticky I could hardly hold the pencil. . . . No exam since – not 'O' or 'A' level or even Degree exams – has had such a terrifying build up and carried with it such a load. (Sue Taylor, b. 1945 – she sat the 11+ in 1956)

Secondary School

In the vast majority of areas in England and Wales secondary schools were clearly divided into grammar schools, where the "academic" children went, and secondary modern schools, which were expected to provide a more practical education for those "not suited" to academic work. In grammar schools pupils usually stayed on until the age of 16 when they took Ordinary Level, and many remained until 18. The school leaving age was 15 and most secondary modern pupils left school after four years, though increasingly towards the end of the '50s a fifth year of education began to be provided in the secondary modern school.

DERBY EDUCATION COMMITTEE

THE MARKEATON SCHOOL FOR GIRLS

SCHOOL REPORT

DECEMBER 1963

Name JOYCE LOWE   Age 14 years 10 months

Form IV i   Average Age 14 years 9 months

Attendances possible 122   Times absent —

Times late — } Excellent.

Honour Marks A   Discredits —

SUBJECT	GRADE	Average Grade	REMARKS
Arithmetic	B	C	Good
Art	C	B	Tries hard.
Craft			
Domestic Subjects	C	B	Must concentrate all the time
English :—			
1. Reading	A	B	
2. Spelling	B	B	Has worked well
3. Writing	C	C	during the term.
4. General	C	B	J.a.B.
5. Literature			
French			
Geography	C	B	} Class work is better than these
History	C	B	} grades indicate.
Music	B	B	Always does her best.
Needlework	A	H	Very good. Shows keen interest
Physical Training	B	C	Good. Neat and alert
Science	B	B	Good.
Scripture	C	B	
Swimming			Good team work done.

RESULT 68° C 7°/° B A very satisfactory report in both work and conduct

Conduct and Progress:— Good — a very pleasant member of the form.

WHAT THE GRADES MEAN:—
A = 85 — 100% — VERY GOOD INDEED
B = 70 — 84% — GOOD
C = 50 — 69% — FAIRLY GOOD
D = 30 — 49% — WEAK
E = Below 30% — VERY WEAK

Form Mistress's Signature D M Maunprice

Headmistress's Signature D M Nicholson

Parent's Signature D Lowe

The Markeaton School was a secondary modern. What differences do you notice between the subjects on the report and those you can do in school today?

First-year pupils at Llwyn-y-Bryn. ▷ School uniforms were traditional and strictly enforced. Compare the way the grammar school pupils are dressed with the secondary modern pupils on page 8. Do you think this difference was important? Explain your answer.

THE NEW SECONDARY MODERNS

One of the advantages of the new system was that where new secondary schools had to be built to accommodate the growing numbers of children, facilities were provided which had been non-existent in the old elementary schools:

On the 13th May the Oldborough Manor County Secondary School [was] opened in the Maidstone Division. . . . The building provides accommodation . . . for 720 pupils in 18 classrooms, wood and metalwork shops, two art and craft rooms, two needlework rooms, two domestic science rooms, which include individual kitchenettes, a science laboratory, science lecture room, library, small hall, large hall and gymnasium. . . . The natural beauty of the site has been enhanced by a well thought out scheme of planting and laying down to grass. . . . Gardening and rural science will occupy a prominent place at the school, which will serve not only the growing housing areas of the south of Maidstone but also the surrounding villages . . . (*Kent Education Gazette*, June 1953)

If you know someone born before 1930 who attended an elementary school, ask them what sort of facilities they had and compare it with the list above.

OUT OF SCHOOL ACTIVITIES

Extract from the Head Girl's Diary, Llwyn-y-Bryn School for Girls, Swansea (a grammar school):

School Year 1955-56
5th October. The Venerable J.J.A. Thomas, M.A., Vicar of Swansea and Archdeacon of Gower, addressed S.C.M. members from the four grammar schools in the Hall. Canon J.J.A. Thomas examined the religious background of Apartheid in South Africa.
6th October. The Reading Circle met in the Hall to listen to a reading of Ibsen's "The Doll's House".
13th October. At the first meeting this year of the Scientific Society the L.VI Science gave very interesting papers on various chemical, physical and botanical subjects.
20th October. A meeting of the Music Society was held in the Hall, at which members were entertained by various gramophone records.
27th October. At a meeting of the History Club, held in the dinner hour, some members of the Upper VI Arts gave papers on Cyprus and the Middle East.

Fashion

The 1950s saw a transformation in fashion and dress styles. In the early years of the decade dress was still influenced by wartime economies and shortages but by the mid-1950s man-made fabrics were becoming increasingly available and the Rock 'n' Roll revolution had brought into fashion, for the first time, a quite separate set of styles for young people.

HIGH FASHION, LOW PRICE

The day-into-evening dress is an important product of the present economy trend. It has usually a neat, little, easily detachable jacket or bolero which fits snugly over the skirt to give the impression of a cover-up afternoon dress, but when evening comes it is removed to show a dress that is strapless, or, at best, has tiny shoestring straps . . .

When buying a dress, the practical angle should be the dominating point. Decide on a basic colour, such as navy, black or brown or, better still, grey. There is no end to the way you can ring the changes with collars and cuffs of different colours, gaily patterned scarfs and contrasting belts.

(*Picturegoer*, 28 January 1950)

NYLON STOCKINGS

I paid £1 for a pair of nylons on the market in 1951 – heaven knows where the stall holder got them from. I kept them in a box and you could take them to the dry cleaners to be mended invisibly! They were like gold. (Cora Buckley, b. 1935)

The stocking with the original slenderising seam

Obtainable in the following styles: *308 Rayon medium weight. 361 Rayon and pure silk mixture. 357 Rayon light-weight. 315 Rayon Plated on Lisle.*

Sunflex
CIRCULAR **STOCKINGS**
Of all good Drapers, Stores, etc.

BY THE MAKERS OF TUDOROSE STOCKINGS

Advert from Picturegoer, January 1950.

When I first started work [1956] I bought a sewing machine – a second-hand treadle. It cost £2. Every week I'd buy material to make a dress for the week-end. Material was about 2/6 a yard. They had very full skirts – dirndls they were called. Underneath you wore net and nylon petticoats stiffened with sugar and water. Some had bones in them and you had to be very careful how you sat down! It was much cheaper to make dresses then – dress makers were always busy. (Dorothy Marsh, b. 1940)

Do you think teenagers still have a distinctive style of dress today? In what ways does it differ from children's/adult's clothing?

Well-dressed young men at a dance in 1953.

A teenager on holiday in Blackpool in 1959. Under her finely pleated skirt is a nylon petticoat to help it stick out. Note also the back-combed "bouffant" hair and stiletto-heeled shoes.

Popular Music

We tend to think of pop-music, the top twenty and pop-stars attended by screaming fans only as part of our own generation, or at the very earliest starting in the Rock 'n' Roll era, which began in Britain in 1956. But since 1946, when Radio Luxembourg began transmitting music on records and record request shows such as "Forces Favourites" became popular on BBC Radio, all these had been features of the "pop-scene". The Rock 'n' Roll revolution was less a revolution in record sales and fans' behaviour than a revolution in the music itself and its associated dancing, bringing for the first time to most white ears the improvised, direct black music of Rhythm and Blues and liberating dance from the formal patterns of the ballroom.

FRANKIE VAUGHAN

Frankie Vaughan was a popular British singer of the 1950s. An article in the *Daily Mirror* in 1954, written at the start of his success, commented:

> Like so many singing stars, he is a gramophone product. Vaughan says "I owe a tremendous amount to disc-jockeys like Jack Jackson, Sam Costa, Wilfred Thomas, Jean Metcalfe and to the comperes of Housewives' Choice and Radio Luxembourg."

Jiving at an evening dance session at a school in Birmingham, 1957.

Another famous Frankie of the time was Frankie Laine, an American mega-star:

> **All Slain(e) by their Frankie**
> . . . Laine came to Belle Vue Manchester last night. He sang to 14,000 teenagers. . . . Girls banging each other's heads as Laine sang. . . . Youths screaming above the screams of the girls . . .
> He sang the hit tune, "My Friend", which has a religious theme. Again came the screams until Laine impressed on his fans that they should remain silent during such a song . . .
> The adulation of this man bewilders me. I felt as if I had become mixed up with a crowd of idol worshippers at the shrine of a voice they love and fear.
> (*Daily Dispatch,* 15 October 1954)

THE NEW MUSIC

Vocalists such as Frankie Vaughan and Frankie Laine often sang with full orchestral backing. The new heroes of the second half of the decade – Elvis Presley, Gene Vincent, Cliff Richard and Tommy Steele, to name but a few – sang with guitars and a small backing group of guitars and drums.

You can get some idea of the contrast in styles by comparing the words of Elvis Presley's 1956 hit "Blue Suede Shoes" (a typical 12-bar blues) with Frankie Laine's hit of 1953, "I Believe".

What strikes you most about them?

I BELIEVE
I believe for every drop of rain that falls
A flower grows.

I believe that somewhere in the darkest
  night
A candle glows.
I believe for everyone that goes astray
Someone will come
To show the way.
I believe above the storm each smallest
  prayer
Will still be heard.
I believe that someone in the great
  somewhere
Hears every word.
Every time I hear a new born baby cry
Or touch a leaf
Or see the sky,
Then I know why I believe.

BLUE SUEDE SHOES
One for the money,
Two for the road,
Three to get ready,
Now go cat go
But don't you step on my blue suede
  shoes.
Well you can do anything
But let me over my blue suede shoes.
You can knock me down,
Step on my face,
Slander my name all over the place,
Do anything that you want to do
But honey lay off of them shoes.
You can burn my house,
Steal my car,
Drain my liquor from an old fruit jar
Do anything that you want to do
But honey lay off of my shoes.

Of course, the best way to understand the difference in the music is to try to get hold of some old records and listen to them.

Television

In 1949 two-thirds of the people of Britain had never seen a television working and only 350,000 households owned one. By 1958, on an average Sunday evening, half the adult population of the country were engaged in watching the "tele". In 1950 the *Radio Times* television programmes took up the last two pages of a 40-page issue. By 1959 they took up pages 8-19 of a 48-page issue.

ANDY PANDY FOR TODDLERS

This is an extract from an article that appeared in the same edition of the *Radio Times* (July 1950):

To most of us television is still a marvel, something to stare at in more than one sense; a bright and shining new toy, the inner workings of which are known only to a fcw . . .

For two years now letters have been falling into the box at Alexandra Palace from mothers of the very young. 'Please,' they say, 'please put on something suitable for children of three.'. . . But what to give them?

To meet at least some of their [the toddlers'] demands a new friend is coming to meet them. Andy Pandy will make his bow on Tuesday at 3.45, again on Thursday and on Tuesday and Thursday of the following week. Although Andy Pandy's arms and legs are attached to strings, he is something more than a puppet. He is not a character performing in front of the children, so much as one of themselves. . . . He comes to the screen in a basket, and for the first minute or two . . . is absorbed in his own affairs. Not until the children have had time to get used to him will he look up and wave . . .

It is hoped that they will be drawn in to take part in and do what he does, following his simple movements, or better still to react freely in response. . . . The four programmes will be regarded as experimental, and television will welcome any comments from mothers.

A DAY'S VIEWING

Television programmes for Tuesday, 11 July 1950:

10-12am: Demonstration film
3pm: "Your Wardrobe", A fashion programme
3.30pm: "Lake of Lucerne", A travel film
3.45-4.00pm: "Andy Pandy", A programme for the very young
8.00pm: "Country Visit": Television Sheep Dog Trial
8.30pm: "October Horizon", A Play by Lydia Ragosin
10-10.15pm: News (sound only)

Note how long television is on the air. There was no ITV until 1955.

CHILDREN'S TV, 1959

On Tuesday, 5 June 1959, the BBC televised the following programmes specifically for children:

11.20-11.45: For the Schools: "Science and Life"

2.5pm: For the Schools: "A Tale of Two Cities" by Charles Dickens

2.35-2.50pm: Watch with Mother: "Andy Pandy"

5.00-6.00pm: Children's Television:

    5.0-5.30: "A Summer in Sicily": A film tour of the ancient splendours of Sicily

    5.30-6.0: "Heidi" by Joanna Spyri: episode four (of six)

Compare these programmes (and those for children in 1950) with a Tuesday's viewing for children today.

Was *Andy Pandy* a success?

Look closely at these two advertisements for television sets. The G.E.C. set was advertised in the Radio Times *in 1950, the Ferguson one in a local paper in 1958. What changes have taken place?*

The Cinema

We used to go to the cinema three times a week. The best seats were 2/3, then 1/9 and 1/6. There were lots and lots of cinemas. Some of them changed their programme three times a week. My favourite film stars were Clark Gable, Esther Williams – she was a swimmer and then a film star and used to appear in those films with water ballets – Bob Hope and Bing Crosby in 'The Road' films. We used to have a serial before the Pathe News. It was a good night out at the pictures. (Jenny Lee, b. 1934)

Although television became increasingly popular through the 1950s, the cinema remained high on the list of favourite entertainments. It was a regular outing for young people – both children who attended Saturday programmes specially screened for them and young adults who did most of their courting in cinemas!

NEW RELEASES

In April 1955 the following films were released to British cinemas:

The Night My Number Came Up
Conquest of Space
As Long As They're Happy
Bullet For Joey
Deep In My Heart
The Adventures of Hajji Baba
Bad Day At Black Rock
Carmen Jones
The Country Girl
The Eternal Sea
Green Fire
A Prize of Gold
That Lady
Vera Cruz
The End Of The Affair
Foxfire
The Long Grey Line
Raising A Riot
Underwater
Young At Heart.

How many of these films or film stars have you or your parents heard of?

MARLON BRANDO

Marlon Brando in the film On the Waterfront, *released in 1954, for which he won an Oscar. It was one of the best American films of the 1950s.*

THEATRE ROYAL Hyde

Phone 2206

Continuous Monday to Saturday from 6 p.m. Matinee Tuesday 2-15 Pensioners' Tuesday Matinee and Thursday Evening Reduced, Price 6d.

Sunday, June 29th. Rock Hudson, Yvonne de Carlo SEA DEVILS Tech. Also QUEST FOR THE LOST CITY Pathe Colour.

Monday, June 30th. 3 Days. Great DOUBLE Comedy Show!
Dirk Bogarde, Brigitte Bardot | Alec Guinness, Peter Sellers

DOCTOR AT SEA (U) | THE LADYKILLERS (U)

VistaVision Technicolor | Technicolor

At 5-40 and 8-55 p.m. | At 7-20 p.m. only.

Thursday, July 3rd for THREE DAYS.

DIRK BOGARDE, DOROTHY TUTIN, CECIL PARKER

A TALE OF TWO CITIES (U)

WITH A CAST OF THC

HIPPODROME Hyde

Tel. 2215

MATINEES MONDAY and THURSDAY at 2 p.m.
MONDAY to SATURDAY CONTINUOUS from 5-45
SUNDAY CONTINUOUS from 5 p.m.

Sunday, June 29th for One Day. Alan Ladd HELL IN FRISCO BAY. Also John Wayne ISLAND IN THE SKY.

Monday, June 30th for THREE DAYS.
Tom Drake, William Hartnell | Kathryn Grant, William Leslie

A DATE WITH DISASTER (U) | THE NIGHT THE WORLD EXPLODED (U)

3-15, 6-55, 9-20. | 2-0, 5-40 7-58.

Thursday, July 3rd for THREE DAYS.
JANE POWELL, GEORGE NADER

FEMALE ANIMAL (A)

CinemaScope 3-20, 6-0 9-0.

Gogi Grant, William Reynolds THE BIG BEAT 2-0, 7-25 Colour.

CHILDREN'S MATINEE THIS SATURDAY at 2-0.

RITZ HYDE

Monday, June 30th. Six Days. Cont. 2 p.m. L

'Spine-Chilling Tension . . . Pluck up courage AND GO!"
Donald Zec—Daily Mirror

CHASE A CROOKED SHADOW

RICHARD TODD, ANNE BAXTER, HERBERT LOM

2-20, 5-35, 8-55. (U).

DAVID BRIAN, MARSHA HUNT

NO PLACE TO HIDE

Colour 4-15, 7-30. (U)

Sunday, June 29th. Continuous 5 p.m. Glenn Ford THE AMERICANO Tech. (U). Robert Stack EAGLE SQUADRON (A)

Hyde's cinemas, June 1958 (population 31,000). About how many films could you see in a year in Hyde in the 1950s?

Although for many families an annual holiday was still beyond their resources, more and more families throughout the 1950s had a week or a fortnight away from home in the summer. At the top end of the scale the number of Britons going abroad for holidays had reached twice its pre-war level by 1958. The touring holiday – taking the car and stopping at farm-houses, inns and hotels for bed and breakfast – was increasingly popular as the numbers of families with cars went up. The seaside was still the favourite place to go and for thousands of families and young people the best and cheapest way to have a holiday by the sea was to go either to a boarding house or to a holiday camp. The 1950s were the boom years for "campers".

Advert from a local paper, March 1953. Which of the activities shown here appeals to you most?

HOLIDAYS RECALLED

I don't remember it as being important. Not like today – no one asked where you'd been when you went back to school. Once every three years we went to relatives. My uncle moved to Brighton when I was eleven, which was very kind of him as I'd never seen the sea until we went to stay with him. Other years, when we didn't go away, we used to go on day trips on a Midland Red coach from Warwick, where I lived. We'd go to places like Wicksteed Park near Northampton, where they had swings and slides, Bourton-on-the-Water, Weston-super-Mare or Rhyl. Staying anywhere, except with relatives, was something we just couldn't afford. (Sue Bush, b. 1943)

Barry Helliwell and his friends at Butlin's in 1953, wearing their House rosettes.

Towards the end of the 1940s we went by train to a place near Cromer and had a week in a caravan by the sea but in the early 50s we got a car and after that we toured and did bed and breakfast. I remember we went to Devon. (Paul Bush, b. 1941)

In 1954, on my 21st birthday, we went abroad. It was a coach trip. We had ten days in France and Belgium and it cost £28. We needed another holiday when we got back because we'd spent so much time just rushing around from place to place trying to see everything. (Shirley Dewsnap, b. 1933)

Factories would dock a bit off your wages every week – 6d or 1/–, to save to your holidays. Around here [Manchester] you didn't have a choice when you took them. You went in Wakes week when everything shut down – shops and schools as well. (Dorothy Marsh, b. 1941)

Do a survey in your class and find out what the most popular holiday is among your age-group now. Have ideas about holidays changed a great deal since the 1950s?

GOOD MORNING CAMPERS

On arrival each camper was allocated a House (like school) and during your week's holiday you would be expected to participate in all the entertainment programmes to try and win points for your house. Houses usually took the names of Royalty, i.e. Gloucester, Kent, Windsor, Connaught etc., and rosettes were worn to denote which House you supported. Good humoured banter was much in evidence. Prizes were given to winners of competitions and often during the evening meal times the progress of your House was announced to loud groans and cheers. During meal times (there was no self-catering) a huge wheel would be spun to see which table won a bottle of champagne. In the 1950s this was the height of opulence.

Entertainment was programmed throughout the day: Swimming Galas, House Football Matches, Treasure Hunts, Dances, Fancy Dress, Knobbly Knees Competitions etc. Campers threw themselves into all these activities with gusto, everything was free to enter and people were determined to enjoy themselves. Perhaps the memories of war were still fresh and peace had created a period of released tension. (Barry Helliwell, Butlin's Camper in 1953)

In 1983 the closure of a number of seaside Holiday Camps was announced. Why do you think they have lost their popularity?

Sport

My mum and dad had this little 9" television set that we watched the Coronation on but there was a great football match that year too; the cup final with Stanley Matthews in it and we got the television for that too. (Cora Buckley, b. 1934)

The *Daily Telegraph,* 4 May 1953:

Blackpool 4   Bolton Wanderers 3 Coronation year cup will be remembered for all time as the match Stanley Matthews won. . . .

Quite apart from the Matthews' masterpiece, there has never been a Wembley final to match this one. It began with the drama of Lofthouse's first minute goal and ended with Perry's last minute match-winner for Blackpool. . . .

"Come on, Stanley!" yelled the crowd – and the magnificent Matthews did not let his audience down. Only one minute was left and again he flashed along the right wing. . . . Instead of passing square he dribbled the ball along the line almost to the goalpost. Then, ever so gently, he touched it back to the onrushing Perry and into the back of the net it flashed. Matthews (and Blackpool) had won the cup at the third time of asking in circumstances as dramatic as any final has ever produced. . . .

The gate receipts of £49,900 set up a new British Record.
(Frank Coles, football reporter)

By the end of the 1950s the five-day working week was widely established. More leisure time meant that more people could pursue hobbies, and participation in sporting activities such as boating and football reached new heights. Although attendance at football matches began to decline towards the end of the decade, it was still watched by millions of people every Saturday and its greatest players were the popular heroes of the day.

A cricket score card, 1959. Cricket in England was still rigidly divided into "gentlemen" – the gifted, often upper-class amateurs; and "players" – the professional members of the team, just as gifted but not so privileged. Can you tell which are the players and which the gentlemen in these teams?

The Hague Bar Junior School Football Team, 1953-54. Note their heavy studded football boots and the real leather football. This got very heavy if the ground was wet and heading it was extremely difficult.

This card does not necessarily include the fall of the last wicket

 4ᴰ **LORD'S** **GROUND** **4**ᴰ

MIDDLESEX v. SUSSEX

Saturday, Monday & Tuesday, May 16, 18 & 19, 1959   (3-day Match)

	MIDDLESEX	First Innings	Second Innings
1	Gale, R. A.		
2	Russell, W. E.		
3	Parfitt, P. H.		
4	Robertson, J. D.		
5	White, R. A.		
6	Titmus, F. J.		
*7	Murray, J. T.		
8	Tilly, H. W.		
†9	J. J. Warr		
10	Hurst, R. J.		
11	Moss, A. E.		

B , l-b , w , n-b ,   B , l-b , w , n-b ,

Scoring rate per over   Total ......220......   Total ....

FALL OF THE WICKETS
1— 2— 3— 4— 5— 6— 7— 8— 9— 10—220
1— 2— 3— 4— 5— 6— 7— 8— 9— 10—

ANALYSIS OF BOWLING	1st Innings						2nd Innings					
Name	O.	M.	R.	W.	Wd.	N-b	O.	M.	R.	W.	Wd.	N-b

No. of balls

	SUSSEX	First Innings	Second Innings
1	Oakman, A. S. M.		
2	Lenham, L. J.		
3	Suttle, K. G.		
*4	Parks, J. M.		
5	Smith, D. V.		
6	E. R. Dexter		
7	Cooper, G. C.		
8	Thomson, N. I.		
9	Bell, R. V.		
†10	R. G. Marlar		
11	Bates, D. L.		

B , l-b , w , n-b ,   B , l-b , w , n-b ,

Scoring rate per over   Total ....   Total ....

FALL OF THE WICKETS
1— 2—70 3— 71 4—80 5— 6— 7— 8— 9— 10—
1— 2— 3— 4— 5— 6— 7— 8— 9— 10—

ANALYSIS OF BOWLING	1st Innings						2nd Innings					
Name	O.	M.	R.	W.	Wd.	N-b	O.	M.	R.	W.	Wd.	N-b

No. of balls

Umpires—J. S. Buller & A. E. Rhodes   Scorers—E. H. Hendren & G. Washer
† Captain   * Wicket-keeper
Play begins at 11.30 each day
Stumps drawn 1st and 2nd days at 6.30, 3rd day at 6
(Half-an-hour extra on the last day if necessary)
Spectators are requested not to enter or leave their seats during the progress of an over

MIDDLESEX WON THE TOSS

Angry Young Men

Towards the end of the 1950s a number of novels were published such as *Room at the Top* by John Braine, *Lucky Jim* by Kingsley Amis and *A Kind of Loving* by Stan Barstow, which told their stories directly, sometimes harshly — their heroes and heroines often working-class and so lacking in "traditional virtues", such as good manners, that they were called "anti-heroes". The books were honest and dealt with subjects considered improper and even indecent — resentment, jealousy, boredom and ambition as well as sexual love. This group of authors were called the "Angry Young Men" and the most famous of them was the playwright John Osborne, whose play *Look Back in Anger,* produced at the Royal Court theatre in 1956, began the controversy.

Look Back in Anger

by

John Osborne

Cast in order of appearance :

Jimmy Porter	Kenneth Haigh
Cliff Lewis	Alan Bates
Alison Porter	Mary Ure

*by Courtesy of Tennent Productions Ltd.
and London Film Productions Ltd.*

Helena Charles	Helena Hughes
Colonel Redfern	John Welsh

The action of the play takes place in the Porter's one-room flat in a large Midland town.

ACT I
Early evening one Sunday in April.

ACT II
Scene 1 : Evening, two weeks later.
Scene 2 : The following evening.

ACT III
Scene 1 : Sunday evening, several months later.
Scene 2 : A few minutes later.

There will be two 12 minute intervals.

The cast list from the original programme.

THE NEW THEATRE

In setting the scene at the opening of the play, John Osborne describes the leading character, Jimmy Porter:

> ... we find that Jimmy is a tall, thin young man about twenty-five, wearing a very worn tweed jacket and flannels. Clouds of smoke fill the room from the pipe he is smoking. He is a disconcerting mixture of sincerity and cheerful malice, of tenderness and freebooting cruelty; restless, importunate, full of pride, a combination which alienates the sensitive and insensitive alike. Blistering honesty, or apparent honesty, like his, makes few friends. To many he may seem insensitive to the point of vulgarity. To others, he is simply a loudmouth.

REVIEWS OF THE PLAY

The *Guardian*, 9 May 1956:

> It is by no means a total success artistically, but it has enough tension, feeling and originality of theme and speech ... it must have woken echoes in anyone who has not forgotten the frustrations of youth.
>
> Mr. Osborne's hero, a boor, a self-pitying, self-dramatising intellectual rebel ... will not be thought an edifying example of chivalry. But those who have not lost the power to examine themselves will probably find something basically true in the prolix shapeless study of a futile frustrated wretch. ... I believe [the English Stage Company] have got a potential playwright at last.

The *Times*, 9 May 1956:

> This play has passages of good violent writing, but its total gesture is altogether inadequate. ...
>
> The piece consists largely of angry tirades. The hero regards himself, and clearly is regarded by the author, as the spokesman for the younger post-war generation which looks round at the world and finds nothing right with it. He shares his squalid Bohemia with his wife and good-natured friend who helps him to run a sweet-shop, and it is easy to understand that his restless disgruntlement, expressed in set pieces of great length and ferocity, must sooner or later make the place too uncomfortable for his companions. ...
>
> The wife is the first to go and the wonder is that she ever comes back.

The *Observer*, 13 May 1956:

> [It] presents post-war youth as it really is, with special emphasis on the non-U intelligentsia ... a minor miracle. All the qualities are there, qualities one had despaired of ever seeing on the stage. ... It is the best young play of its decade.

All these reviewers were eye-witnesses of the same performance of the play. How do you account for their different reactions?

National Service: Joining Up

1945-61 is the only period in British history where men were compelled to serve in the armed forces in peacetime. Many other countries had (and still have) compulsory military training, but there was always a resistance in Britain to the idea of compelling anyone into the services and this was only reluctantly overcome even in wartime. On the other hand, some people have always seen national service as a desirable thing – teaching discipline and respect and being a good way to "make a man of you".

National Service grade card.

NATIONAL SERVICE ACTS

GRADE CARD

Registration No. *DFN 49317*

Mr. *Barry Helliwell.*

whose address on his registration card is

11 Carlton Av.

Shelton Lock Derby

was medically examined at *DERBY*

and placed in GRADE* *I (One)*

on *3. V. 55*

Chairman of Board *John B. Grove*

Medical Board Stamp *DERBY*

Man's Signature *B Helliwell*

* The roman numeral denoting the man's Grade (with number also spelt out) will be entered in RED ink by the Chairman himself, e.g., Grade I (one), Grade II (two) (a) (Vision).

N.S.55. [P.T.O.

DESCRIPTION OF MAN

Date of birth *30.3.37.*

Height *5* ft *6¾* ins.

Colour of eyes *Blue*

Colour of hair *Auburn*

If before you are called up for service you have any serious illness or serious accident, or have reason to think there has been a deterioration in your health, you should immediately inform the Local Office of the Ministry of Labour and National Service whose address appears on the back of your registration form N.S.2, giving full particulars, including any medical evidence you can supply, and quoting your Registration No. and other entries made on form N.S.2, so that the information can be considered before an enlistment notice is issued to you.

If this Certificate is lost or mislaid, the fact must be at once reported.

The finder should send it to the nearest Local Office of the Ministry of Labour and National Service.

(1384) 455414 43846/D1191 100M 9/54 SP/TBH **Gp.38**

No. 24 PRIMARY TRAINING CENTRE.

SPECIAL
Certificate of Training.

This is certify that No. ___21037846___ Rank ___Pte___ Name ___DAVIES G.___

(i) Obtained a score of ___76___ out of 80 points in the Rifle Course Part I.

And a score of ___101___ out of 110 points in the L.M.G. Course Part I.

(ii) Was recommended by his Platoon Commander as one of the ___THREE___ best men in his Platoon at Drill and Turnout.

(iii) Passed Tests of Elementary Training in Rifle and L.M.G. and has been awarded this Certificate at the end of his Primary Training.

Lt.-Col.,
Commanding No. 24 Primary Training Centre.

DATE ___12/12/47___

F. H. JONES Printer. Street. BRECON.

Certificate of training.

GENERAL MILITARY TRAINING

I was at Boddington when I was called up. I was instructed to call at a place in Coventry for a medical examination and where a decision would be made on which branch of the forces I was to join. It turned out there were only vacancies in the army so on 6th November 1947 I reported to Brecon Barracks to begin 6 weeks of General Military Training (G.M.T.). This consisted mainly of drill and weapons training. My overriding impression of these first 6 weeks was of doing things but never knowing why. If you asked for an explanation you either got "sat on" or ignored. Consequently I went around in a state of bewilderment. I can best illustrate this by telling you of the certificate which was to be awarded to the best recruit. My intake consisted of 72 men split into 2 platoons of 36. We were told that at the end of our training there would be a passing out parade held before the G.O.C. Western Command and on that day he would award a special certificate to the outstanding recruit – well, to cut a long story short I won the certificate and to this day I am completely baffled as to how I came to win it! (Graham Davies, The Life Guards, 1947-49)

Army National Service recruits on General Military Training. Brecon Barracks, 1947.

What do you think the Army might have been looking for in its best recruits?

National Service: Serving Your Time

Many men found National Service an interesting interlude in the business of living – something you observed rather than participated in, but their recollections of life in the services are often vivid and amusing. The experience bore little or no direct relevance to the careers and occupations the men were to pursue in civilian life, but few of them actively regret their time in uniform.

THE ROYAL NAVY

After basic training during which one learnt the routine and discipline of the Navy, I was posted to a destroyer, H.M.S. *Savage*, where we put into practice the various skills of seamanship we had learned.

Thus I came to spend November in the North Sea in very rough weather. There for the first time I learnt what being on watch meant. Ships have to be manned continuously every hour of the day and so the crew is divided into groups, each of which has four-hour duties in addition to one's normal work. The watch I found the worst was the Midnight to 4am largely because it broke up one's sleep. . . .

I was posted to Gosport in Hampshire where I joined H.M. Coastal Forces. There I worked on Motor Torpedo Boats. . . . The crews on these boats were very small, numbering only about six, and the atmosphere was much more relaxed and friendly. At sea we wore white sweaters, jeans and plimsolls and we took turns cooking in the galley.

So, compared with many, my National Service was fairly relaxed and much less severe than that experienced by some of my friends who were fighting terrorists in Malaya or taking part in the Suez campaign. However, I was very pleased to finish my two years for I am not a practical person and knots and cables always caused me problems. As my final testimonial said, "This rating will be happier when he can use his mind rather than his hands." I heartily agreed. (Michael Rawcliffe, RN 1955-57, now a history teacher)

10

ANY ADDITIONAL INFORMATION AND TYPE OF EMPLOYMENT FOR WHICH RECOMMENDED :—

Cpl. Helliwell has carried out his duties in a satisfactory manner. He has been employed on work requiring a certain amount of detailed investigation and accuracy.

He is considered not suitable for employment on work of a clerical nature.

(Signature of Commanding Officer)
(S. M. RAVENHILL)
(NAME IN BLOCK LETTERS)

Rank Sqn Ldr.   Date 28 · 4 · 58

No. 13 M.U.
-8 MAY 1958
STAFFORD

◁ *A page from the Royal Air Force Certificate of Service of Barry Helliwell.*

Barry Helliwell (left), RAF Hereford, July 1955. Barry Helliwell is now a social worker.

LIFE IN THE ARMY

The things that stick out in my mind are the filthy living conditions in the Barracks – blankets never washed – only shaken. We had blanket shaking parades. You paraded with your blankets and on a certain command you turned about and faced the man behind you when you first shook his blankets and then ... yours. Needless to say you were enveloped in a cloud of dust. ...

Every few weeks you did a guard duty. At about 10.30pm someone went to the cookhouse and collected a bucket of cocoa. This was brought back to the guardroom where it was placed on top of the "smokey joe" stove for the remainder of the night. When the guard was changed everyone coming off guard "dunked" his mug into the bucket for a cup of cocoa and at the same time someone would stir up the stove so that a cloud of dust rose up and then fell back onto the cocoa. By the morning it was a most peculiar colour and tasted like nothing on earth."

(Graham Davies, now a farmer)

Imagine you are a National Serviceman on watch or guard duty. Describe your thoughts about your time in the services. Are you pleased about it? Is it boring or are you learning something worthwhile? Why are you doing it?

Suez

In November 1956 British and French troops invaded Egypt and their aeroplanes bombed Cairo. The aim of the attack was to regain control of the Suez Canal which had been nationalized (taken over) by the Egyptian government. The excuse for the action was the attack on Egypt by Israel, which, Britain and France argued, put the vital waterway in jeopardy. The British and French reaction aroused a storm of controversy at home and abroad. The United States refused to support her allies and in Britain feeling was deeply divided between those who supported the government's action and those who opposed it. The Prime Minister at the time was Sir Anthony Eden.

SUEZ RECALLED

From time to time, there arises a dispute on matters so fundamental and involving such deep feelings as to cause temporary, and even permanent, rifts between old friends, divisions in families, heavy stresses on Party organisations, and implicating not merely those normally affected by political controversy but the whole mass of the population. Such emotions were caused by Munich and, nearly twenty years later, by Suez. . . .

In the few hours during which I could escape from the precincts of Whitehall, I observed that these acrimonious disputes had spread into premises where they are rarely found – in the clubs, in the pubs, in the streets, in the Underground. Wherever men congregated the argument was strenuously conducted – sometimes with courtesy and in polite language but more often in homely and simple terms. The prevailing rancour spread to private homes and continued long after the end of the immediate crisis. As at Munich, personal quarrels disturbed the equanimity of private life, and in some cases, as I know to my own sorrow, led to permanent estrangement of old friends. (Harold Macmillan, Chancellor of the Exchequer at the time of Suez, in his autobiography, *Riding the Storm*, 1971.)

FROM A GOVERNMENT SUPPORTER

Sir, Although I do not belong to your political school, I have always been a great admirer of the "Guardian". But the attitude that you have taken up against the Government ever since Nasser nationalised the Suez Canal Company, and more latterly still your furious and almost hysterical editorials, has exceeded all bounds. I can no longer tolerate your paper in my home and have stopped my subscription . . .
Yours, etc . . .
(*Manchester Guardian*, 5 November 1956)

DEMONSTRATIONS

The *Manchester Guardian*, Monday, 5 November 1956:

WILD SCENES IN WHITEHALL
27 Arrests: 8 Policemen Hurt

Many thousands of demonstrators blocked Whitehall for nearly an hour last evening, sporadically chanting "Eden must go", "Resign", and, after mounted police had turned them back from Downing Street, "Shame". For the first fifteen minutes there were repeated scuffles and a few fights with the police....

For most of the hour that Whitehall was occupied, masses of people waved banners stating "Into the Canal with Eden". "No war over Suez". "Respect the United Nations". Occasionally sections roared in unison "Down with Eden" and "Eden must go". Whitehall echoed with cheering and booing, and hundreds of feet and hands drummed on a corrugated iron hoarding.

Telegram to the *Manchester Guardian,* 5 November 1956:

Sir, – Suggest you give editorial support immediately campaign proposing all opponents Government Suez policy wear black tie till cease-fire- HARRY PITT, Worcester College, Oxford.

Why do you think people felt so strongly about "Suez"?

LOCAL ATTITUDES

For some people Suez had a different significance:

I'd just started work at a textile factory. Textile firms were closing down and we were frightened that the cotton wouldn't get through. It put pressure on because everyone was frightened for their jobs and worried more mills would close because we wouldn't get the cotton through the canal from India and Egypt. (Dorothy Marsh, from Manchester)

. . . and a domestic consequence:

We didn't arrange to go on holiday that year because they said petrol would be rationed. They issued the coupons in December. (Shirley Dewsnap, b. 1933)

The weight of international opinion was heavily against Britain too and before the year was out, British troops had withdrawn. In the new year Sir Anthony Eden resigned as Prime Minister and was replaced by Harold Macmillan.

Find the Suez Canal on a map. Why do you think it is such an important water-way? Find out who controls the Suez Canal today.

Health

The introduction of the National Health Service in 1947 was probably the most important act of the reforming Labour Government of 1945-51. Medical care was to be financed through taxation and all charges for medical services were abolished. This removed anxiety from millions of families and, coinciding as it did with new revolutions in medicine and surgery, made accessible to the whole population a level of medical care previously unimagined. Children's clinics were established where the health and progress of pre-school children were monitored. Dental care was freely provided for school children and the health of the nation improved significantly during the decade.

PAYING YOUR WAY

I can remember having to pay to go to the doctor's. The doctor's man used to come round and collect your money every week. I can remember my aunt had to pay out of her pension which was 10/– a week. And then suddenly you didn't have to pay any more. You could even have new glasses for free. They were awful – the glasses – but they were free. It took a lot of worry away. Like if all the children had measles at the same time you could call the doctor without having to worry about the bills. (Cora Buckley, b. 1934)

NEW TECHNIQUES

Evelyn Prentis returned to nursing in the early 1950s after a break of only a few years. She describes some of the changes she encountered:

It was almost twenty years since I had done my training, and I was as much of an old-timer as I was a part-timer. I had been taught to cosset pneumonia with poultices and to bring abscesses to a painful head with fomentations. Now there was a magic wand being waved over everything which had made the poultices and fomentations as old-fashioned as leeches and cupping. The wand was called antibiotics. . . .

"We never seem to do any proper nursing," I grumbled to Brown one morning when we were in the medical room boiling up a fresh lot of syringes for the next lot of injections. . .

"What are you talking about?" asked Brown. . .

"Well, at least we used to nurse people when there weren't any antibiotics," I said. . . . . "All we seem to do these days is stick needles into people. I sometimes feel more like a technician than a nurse."

"I don't agree with you," she said. . . . "It's still nursing. We do it in a different way, that's all, and a lot better way, in my opinion. Think of the women on the gynae wards who used to die of septicaemia and puerperal fever, and the breast abscesses and the pneumonias, and the weeks it took to clear up little things like an ear infection and the simple things that children used to die of." (Evelyn Prentis, *A Nurse in Parts*, Hutchinson, 1980)

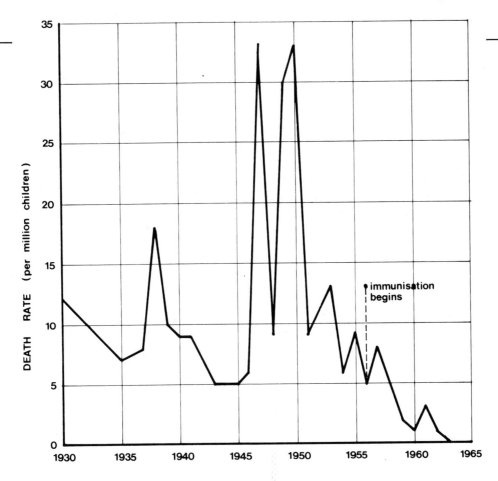

YEAR

Graph showing the decline in the annual death rate from polio of children under 15 in England and Wales. How quickly did the vaccine take effect? Were there any major outbreaks of polio after 1956?

Poliomyelitis is a crippling and often fatal disease which seems particularly to affect children. It is virtually unheard-of in Britain today, as most people have been immunized against it. The vaccine was first developed in 1954.

Make a list of all the medicines you have taken this year. Try to find out which would have been available before 1950.

Science and Space Exploration

It was in the 1950s that what we often now call the new industrial revolution began. In the early years of the decade British scientists built the first commercial computers – dinosaur-like in their size and capability, but necessary fore-runners of the micro-technology now part of our everyday lives. A group of scientists meeting in 1950, however, failed to hold out any hope of successfully exploring beyond the earth's atmosphere before the end of the century. By the end of the decade satellites had circled the earth, the other side of the moon had been photographed and within eighteen months man would be journeying in space, too. Is it possible to say which of the breakthroughs described here was the more important?

The Fiction: Dan Dare was the most famous Space Pilot in the early 1950s. He was the leading character in the Eagle *comic and rather like a wartime RAF pilot! This is a page from a story called "Dan Dare, Pilot of the Future, in 'Operation Plum Pudding'".*

THE FACT

On 4 October 1957 the Soviet Union successfully launched their first satellite. The word "sputnik" became part of the English language overnight and hundreds of people searched the night sky for the star that wasn't a star. The headlines in the *Manchester Guardian* on 5 October read:

THE FIRST EARTH SATELLITE

**Russian's Success:
circling world every 95 minutes
RADIO SIGNALS HEARD**

On 7 October the paper commented:

> [The Soviet's] achievement is immense. It demands a psychological adjustment on our part.... to the relationship of the world and what is beyond. The barriers of imagination which most of us erect between ourselves and those distant places where red dust is blown about the surfaces of strange planets, or where there is no sun, no touch, no gravity, nothing, have now been breached. We must be prepared to be told what the other side of the moon looks like or how thick the cloud on Venus might be.

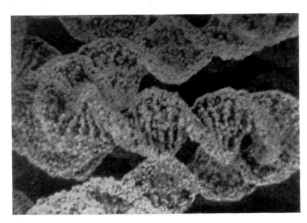

The Double Helix of DNA.

THE SECRET OF LIFE

In the very earth-bound world of genetics, a breakthrough of tremendous importance was made in April 1953, when British and American scientists working together in Cambridge identified and described DNA (deoxyribonucleic acid). DNA is the molecule of heredity, and to know how it works is to know how genetic directions are written and transmitted. DNA is the material of which genes are composed and it is genes which determine the nature of any organism from bacteria to humans. Understanding DNA is a necessary step towards understanding how organisms can go wrong, how viruses work, etc. Much of modern research into cancer is based on an analysis of DNA and how it works.

James Watson was 24 and Francis Crick was 35 when they discovered DNA. Here is part of the story from James Watson's book, *The Double Helix*:

> When I got to our still empty office the following morning, I quickly cleared away the papers from my desk top so that I would have a large, flat surface on which to form pairs of bases held together by hydrogen bonds.... Suddenly ... all the hydrogen bonds seemed to form naturally; no fudging was required to make the two types of base pairs identical in shape....
>
> Upon his arrival Francis did not get more than half way through the door before I let loose that the answer to everything was in our hands. Though as a matter of principle he maintained scepticism for a few moments, the ... pairs had their expected impact.... However, we both knew that we would not be home until a complete model was built in which all the stereo-chemical contacts were satisfactory.... Thus I felt slightly queasy when at lunch Francis winged into the Eagle to tell everyone within hearing distance that we had found the secret of life. (*The Double Helix* by James Watson, Weidenfeld and Nicolson, 1968)

You may have got the impression looking through the book that things were very cheap in those days. But in order to understand the prices of goods, we need to know something about wages, too, and the cost of housing. Though inflation continued throughout the 1950s it never reached double figures and so it is possible to make a rough comparison of prices from the beginning to the end of the decade.

GROCERY PRICES IN 1952

Potatoes	2d per lb
Butter	4s per lb (rationed)
Milk	7d per pint
Meat	2s per lb (rationed)
Bacon	4s per lb (rationed)
Ground rice	1s per lb
Tea	2s 6d per lb
Cigarettes	1s 3½d for 10
Beer	1s 2d per pint

CLOTHES PRICES, 1953

Summer dress	65/11
Raincoat	£3/19/6
Boy's suit	37/6
Man's suit	£3/15/–
Coat	£3/19/6
Skirt	23/11

RENTS AND WAGES, 1952

Average Rent	12/6
Average wage	£7/11/–

Advert from a theatre programme of the mid-1950s.

1956:

Superintendant Midwife required for
the maternity unit.
Salary £670-895.

Lecturer in the Department of Applied
Mathematics.
Salary in the range of £650-1,350

Senior Jig and Tool Designer with
H.N.C. or equivalent.
Salaries ranging from £720 to £850.

1958:

Private secretary:
must be intelligent and well spoken.
Commencing salary according to age
and experience, but not less than
£8/10/– per week.

British Railways:
Require boys of good education for
employment as junior clerks. Salary
(per annum) age 15 or 16 £186 rising
annually to £506 at 28 years.

These advertisements are from newspapers of the time.

ILFORD Sportsman

**The amazing
miniature
that gives you
COLOUR and
black-and-white
... and look how
little it costs!**

No other camera gives you so much for so
little as the 35mm Ilford 'Sportsman.'
Radiant colour pictures . . . crisp black-and-whites . . . the 'Sportsman' does a
wonderful job—and even a beginner can handle it easily.
High-speed Dignar f/3·5 lens and shutter speeds up to 1/200th sec. ensure perfect
pictures in all conditions. Large eye-level viewfinder with luminous guide lines, press-
button release, interlocking film wind and shutter setting to prevent double exposure.
Beautifully styled, the Ilford 'Sportsman' looks like the little masterpiece it is—and
yet it costs only £11.11.11. (Leather ever-ready case, 41/3 extra.)
See this camera at your photo-shop-you won't find better value anywhere. £11.11.11
In summertime use—ILFORD COLOUR FILM 'D' and ILFORD FP 3

To: ILFORD LIMITED, ILFORD, ESSEX
Please send full details of the 'Sportsman' camera

NAME _____

ADDRESS _____

_____ RT

Advert from The Radio Times, *June 1959.*

Imagine you have been employed in one of the
jobs advertised here, and are living in one of
the houses described on pages 10-11. With
careful budgeting, how many of the consumer
goods mentioned in this book could you afford
in two years? Remember, hire purchase was
available on some goods.

__ Difficult Words and Abbreviations __

apartheid	literal meaning: separate development. The word used to describe the policies of the White South African Government towards the majority black and coloured population.
cupping	taking blood by placing a cup over a cut (incision) and drawing it out: an old remedy for a fever.
dep.	deposit.
det.	detached.
drill	marching, saluting.
easy terms	hire purchase; paying a deposit for an article and the balance over a number of months.
fomentation	application of a warm, soft substance (dry or wet) to the body, to relieve pain or inflammation.
G.E.C.	General Electric Company.
G.O.C.	General Officer Commanding.
Great Exhibition	an international exhibition of industry and achievement, held at Crystal Palace in 1851.
gynae	gynaecology; referring to medical and surgical conditions of women's reproductive organs.
H.M.	Her Majesty's.
leeches	leeches were sometimes used to draw blood in old-fashioned medicine.
Lt. Col.	Lieutenant Colonel.
L.M.G.	Light Machine Gun.
M.A.	Master of Arts.
Munich	The meeting in 1938, between Hitler and the British Prime Minister, Neville Chamberlain, that partitioned Czechoslovakia and was supposed to bring peace.
non-U	a phrase meaning not quite acceptable to the establishment.
platoon	smallest unit of men in the army.
poultice	something soft, like bread, mixed with boiling water and spread on linen, then placed on a sore or inflamed spot.
P.T.	purchase tax.
pte.	private.
puerperal fever	an infection suffered by women who had just had a baby. It was quite common and often fatal.
septicaemia	septic poisoning.
Sqn.	squadron.
stereo-chemical	to do with the relative position in space of atoms in a molecule.
S.C.M.	Student Christian Movement.
terr.	terraced.
vitreous enamel	a painted surface that was hard, shiny and easy to clean.

Conversion Table

1d	less than ½p
6d	2½p
1/–	5p
2/6	12½p
5/–	25p
10/–	50p
£1	£1
1 guinea (£1/1/–)	£1.05p
10 guineas (£10/10/–)	£10.50p

Biographical Notes

CRICK, Francis Harry Compton, b. June 1916. Educated at Mill Hill School, University College, London and Caius College, Cambridge. From 1940 to 1947 he was a scientist at the Admiralty and since then has held various academic appointments at Cambridge and Universities in the United States. Since 1977 he has been a professor at the Salk Institute in California USA. He won the Nobel Prize for Medicine in 1962 (with J.D. Watson and M.F.H. Wilkins) for his work on DNA.

EDEN, Anthony Robert, b. 1897. Educated at Eton and Christ Church, Oxford. While serving in the First World War he won the Military Cross. He was MP for Warwick and Leamington constituency from 1923 to 1957. He served as Foreign Secretary from 1935-38 when he resigned over Munich. He was re-appointed Foreign Secretary by Churchill in 1940 and again when the Conservatives returned to power in 1951. He became Prime Minister on Churchill's retirement in 1955 and served in that post until 1957, when he resigned because of ill-health. He was created the Earl of Avon in 1961 and died in 1977.

MACMILLAN, Harold, b. 1894. Educated at Eton and Balliol College, Oxford. He served in the First World War and became MP for Stockton-on-Tees in 1924.

He served as Conservative MP from then until 1929 and again from 1931 to 1945. He then became MP for Bromley, for which constituency he sat until 1964. He was Minister of Housing and Local Government from 1951-54, Minister of Defence from 1954-55, Foreign Secretary in 1955, Chancellor of the Exchequer 1955-57. He became Prime Minister when Sir Anthony Eden resigned and remained Prime Minister until his own resignation because of ill-health in 1964. Since 1960 he has been Chancellor of the University of Oxford. He was created an Earl on his 90th birthday and took his title from his first constituency, becoming Earl of Stockton.

MATTHEWS, Stanley, b. 1915. Educated at Wellington School, Hanley. A professional footballer, he played first for England in 1934 and was capped 55 times. From 1947 to 1961 he played for Blackpool and was in their team which won the FA Cup in 1953. From 1961 to 1965 he played for Stoke City. He was knighted in 1965.

PRESLEY, Elvis, b. 1935 in Tupelo, Mississippi, USA. Leading American and world pop-star. Major hits include "Heartbreak Hotel" (1956), "Blue Suede Shoes" (1956), "Jailhouse Rock" (1958), "It's Now or Never" (1960), "In the Ghetto" (1969). Regarded by many as the "King" of Rock 'n' Roll. He died in Memphis, Tennessee, USA in August 1977, aged 42.

RICHARD, Cliff, b. 1940. Educated at Riversmead School, Chestnut. He is the leading British popular singer and a well-known evangelical Christian. His hits include "Living Doll" (1959), "The Young Ones" (1962), "Congratulations" (1968), "Devil Woman" (1976). He was awarded the OBE in 1980.

WATSON, James Dewey, b. 1928. Educated at the Universities of Chicago and Indiana, USA. Fellow at the Cavendish Laboratory, Cambridge University from 1951-53. Since then he has held a series of academic appointments at American Universities. He won the Nobel Prize for Medicine in 1962 (with Francis Crick and M.F.H. Wilkins) for his work on DNA.

Date List

1950 February: General Election. Labour returned with a reduced majority.

1950-3 Korean War.

1951 May-September: Festival of Britain.
October: General Election. Conservative victory.

1952 February: Death of George VI.

1953 April: DNA described.
June: The Coronation of Queen Elizabeth II. Everest climbed.

1954 May: Roger Bannister runs the mile in less than four minutes.
July: end of rationing.

1955 May: General Election. Conservatives win.
September: ITV begins broadcasting.

1956 "Rock around the Clock" hits the charts.
Immunization against polio begins.
May: *Look Back in Anger* produced at the Royal Court.
October: Suez crisis begins.
November: British and French troops invade Egypt.
December: Troops withdrawn.

1957 January: Sir Anthony Eden resigns as Prime Minister.
October: Soviet Union launches first satellite.

1959 October: General Election. Conservatives win.

Book List

V. Bogdanov and R. Skidelsky (eds.), *The Age of Affluence (1951-1964)* (Macmillan, 1970)

Pauline Gregg, *The Welfare State* (Harrap, 1967)

C.A.R. Hills, *Growing Up in the 1950s* (Batsford, 1983)

Harry Hopkins, *The New Look: A Social History of the 40's and 50's in Britain* (Secker and Warburg, 1963)

Peter Lewis, *The Fifties* (Heinemann, 1978)

Alan Sked and Chris Cook, *Post War Britain: A Political History* (Penguin, 1979)

NORTH
SEA

IRISH SEA

0   50   100
km

Blackpool

Denton Stalybridge
Rhyl Manchester Hyde
Marple Glossop
New Mills Sheffield

Markeaton
Derby

Cromer

Coventry
Warwick Northampton
Hereford Cambridge
Brecon

Swansea

Boddington

Bourton-
on-the-
Water

LONDON

Weston-
super-Mare

Worcester
Park

Maidstone
Boughton
Monchelsea

Gosport

Brighton St Mary's
Bay

Plymouth

E N G L I S H   C H A N N E L

Index